Round Buildings,
Square Buildings &
Buildings That Wiggle Like a Fish

Also by PHILIP M. ISAACSON

A Short Walk Around the Pyramids &
Through the World of Art

Round Buildings,
Square Buildings &
Buildings That Wiggle Like a Fish

BY PHILIP M. ISAACSON

With photographs by the author

EMBER

For Andrew, Sarah, Julia, Jacob, and for Miranda
—P.M.I.

Visit us on the Web! randomhouseteens.com

Educators and librarians, for a variety of teaching tools, visit us at RHTeachersLibrarians.com

The Library of Congress has cataloged the hardcover edition of this work as follows:
Isaacson, Philip M., 1924–2013
Round buildings, square buildings, and buildings that wiggle like a fish.
Summary: Explores various architectural styles around the world depicting churches, fortresses, bridges, air terminals, mills, cliff dwellings, tombs, and lighthouses of particular note.
1. Architecture—Juvenile literature. [1. Architecture.] I. Title.
NA2555.I83 1988 720 87-16967

ISBN 978-0-394-89382-2 (trade) — ISBN 978-0-394-99382-9 (lib. bdg.) — ISBN 978-1-101-93320-6 (pbk.)

MANUFACTURED IN MALAYSIA

10 9 8 7 6 5 4 3 2 1

First Ember Edition 2016

Frontispiece / The granite wall with the round corners is almost all that remains of the Stock Exchange Building at 53 State Street in Boston. The Exchange was built between 1889 and 1891 from designs of Peabody and Stearns. When the glass tower behind it was added from 1981 to 1984, most of the original building was torn down. The tower was designed by WZMH Group. The building, with its new tower, has been renamed Exchange Place.

Tailpiece / The Centre National d'Art et de Culture Georges-Pompidou in Paris opened in 1977. It is an art museum, a place to perform music, a library, and an archive of industrial design. It was designed by two architects, Richard Rogers of England and Renzo Piano of Italy. The Pompidou Center is a glass box six stories high and much longer than a football field. You can hardly see the glass from the outside, however, because the building is covered by a forest of pipes, ducts, and permanent scaffolding. Those tubes, which carry the heating, cooling, and ventilating and electrical systems of the Pompidou Center, have turned it into the largest Erector Set in the world.

Contents

Round Buildings,
Square Buildings &
Buildings That Wiggle Like a Fish

1

Three Wondrous Buildings

This is a building in a small city in northern India (1). People come from all over the world to see it. Many of them come because they feel that it is the most beautiful building in the world. It is called the Taj Mahal and it is a valentine from a great emperor to a wife who died when she was very young. It is made of marble the color of cream. Each afternoon the

2

sun changes the color of the Taj Mahal. First it turns it pink, then yellow, then the color of apricots. In the evening it becomes brown, and when the moon shines on it, it is blue and gray (2). In the moonlight it becomes the old emperor, asleep and dreaming.

The Taj Mahal is about three hundred years old. This building is much older (3, 84). It was built about 2,500 years ago and stands on a

3

white marble hill in Greece. Because it too is made of white marble, it seems to grow out of that hill as though it were a group of great trees standing in a small forest. It is called the Parthenon in honor of an ancient Greek goddess. Though it is made only of marble posts—called columns—and a very simple roof, it is just as famous as the Taj Mahal and has just as many admirers. Many people feel that it is the most beautiful building in the world.

This building is also very famous (4). It is in a French city near Paris called Chartres. Its name is Our Lady of Chartres. One part of it is almost nine hundred years old and so it is older than the Taj Mahal but not nearly as old as the Parthenon. It is made of a hard stone that is not very friendly and has many moods. On a sunny day, with fast-moving clouds behind it, Chartres looks like a great ship sailing along against the sky, but on a dark day it can be cold and gray and a little frightening. Chartres is another building that many people feel is the most beautiful of all.

In many ways these buildings are alike. All of them are places of worship: the Taj Mahal is a mosque, the Parthenon is a temple, Chartres is a church. Each was built in honor of a woman; the Taj Mahal honors a young

4

wife, the Parthenon honors a young goddess, Chartres honors a saint. Finally, all three are very beautiful.

In other ways, however, they're not alike at all. The Taj Mahal sits in a riverside garden with pools of water to reflect its soft shapes. The Parthenon is short and as powerful as a king on a mountain throne. Chartres is hard and sharp with towers tall enough to slice open the sky—towers so tall that you can see them from afar, long before you see the great cathedral beneath them.

These wonderful buildings tell us many things about beauty. First they tell us that there are many kinds of beauty. There is beauty in buildings that look soft and creamy, in buildings that look short and strong, and in buildings that are sharp and tall. They also tell us that all beautiful buildings, indeed all beautiful things, have a magical feeling about them. That feeling is called harmony.

A building has harmony when everything about it—its shape, its walls, its windows and doors—seems just right. Each must be a perfect companion for the other. When each suits the other so well that they come to belong to one another, the building is a work of art. The person who plans such a building—who designs it—is an artist, sometimes a very great artist.

We're going to look at many beautiful buildings to help us understand more about harmony. You've heard of some of the buildings. You may even have seen, or someday will see, some of them. Others are not famous at all and you may never see them. But famous or not, all of them share in the same magic, the magic of harmony.

Old Stones

This is Stonehenge (5). No one really knows how old it is. Some scientists believe it is 3,500 years old; some believe it is much older. We may never discover its true age, but one thing is certain. It is one of the oldest structures—things built by humans—on earth. It sits on Salisbury Plain, a few hours' journey from London. In the early morning, as it steps slowly out of the mist, it is lonely and haunting. For a moment it is an ancient sentinel—a soldier—standing guard over the plain. But as the sun burns the mist away, the great stones arrange themselves into strange circles. Stonehenge may be a huge calendar, a place to watch the travels of the sun, or, perhaps, an outdoor temple of an old and forgotten people. It is a marvelous, sad, and beautiful place, but it is not a building. It does not provide shelter.

Like Stonehenge, this also reminds us of a building (6). Stonehenge is made of simple walls that make circles within circles. This is a long wall with a sharp bend in it. As you can

6

see, however, it is not simple. It is made of small stones laid one on another to form strong, slender arches. The wall is called an aqueduct and, in places, it stands a hundred feet above the ground. It seems to fly between a golden city—a city that sits on a hump shaped like a corn muffin—and a hill almost a half mile away. The aqueduct was built by the Romans twenty centuries ago to carry water to Segovia. Even today, it brings water to that old Spanish city. Trucks rumble through its arches on their way to Madrid, but the old houses of the city still bow down before it.

It took fourteen years to build the Brooklyn
Bridge (7). Finished in 1883, it was, and still
is, a wonder of the world. It joins Manhattan
and Brooklyn, and though it now has two
sisters, it is by far the most beautiful. Like
Stonehenge and the Roman aqueduct, it
embodies ideas about beauty that are very old.
It is supported by two giant stone towers.
They are magnificent. Their shape comes from
both the temples of ancient Egypt and the old
cathedrals of France. The outline of each
tower—the way it moves slowly in and
then pushes out just as it reaches the top—is

Egyptian. The arches in the towers end in the graceful points we find in the taller of the towers at Chartres (4). It is not easy to bring together two ideas about beauty that are as different as ancient Egyptian and old French. Still, the designers of the bridge did so very well. Most bridges are made of concrete and steel and tell us about the power of engineering. The Brooklyn Bridge is not like them; it tells us about the shapes of grand old buildings. It will always be a wonder because of a friendly game it seems to play. Its designers wove webs of light wires and cables and hung them from the towers to hold the bridge's roadways and paths. The fat towers make the webs look silky, and the silky webs make the towers seem even heavier than they are. This game of tag will go on forever.

Here, at last, is a building made of stone, but it is also a bridge, or perhaps a bridge that is also a building (8). It is the Pulteney Bridge at Bath, England, and was built about 1774. To help pay for it, the owner, a gentleman named William Pulteney, asked the designer for two rows of shops, one for each side of the roadway. Because of the rows, you hardly know that you are on a bridge as you walk along it. But from the riverbank you can see lovely arches carrying the shops across the water. The bridge is gentle and quiet. Its smooth stone and delicate shapes speak to one another in soft voices. Those voices—almost whispers—turn Mr. Pulteney's bridge into a short poem.

8

9

This stone bridge in Spain is also part building (9). It is in a mountain town called Ronda and has a three-hundred-year-old prison below its roadway. You can see the prison window just above the middle arch. It is easy to think of the bridge at Bath as a poem, but the bridge at Ronda, called the Puente Nuevo, is very different. It is a battle song and uses mighty arches to cross a deep ravine. Everything about it is thick and solid. It looks strong and it is strong; strong enough to carry the heaviest trucks that roll across Spain.

So we see that two structures made of the same material and that do the same thing—whether they are bridges or buildings—can have very different personalities. They can look gentle and so have a gentle personality; they can look powerful and therefore have a strong personality. Sometimes, like the Brooklyn Bridge, they manage to look both gentle and powerful at the same time. But whatever their personalities, when their parts are in harmony with one another, the structures will be beautiful.

CHAPTER THREE

Thick Walls
and Thin Walls

Walls can be made of many things. The
materials in a wall give the building character
and mood and help us decide how we are
going to feel about it.

    This is called the Flatiron Building (10). It is
a famous building in Manhattan and was built
at the beginning of the last century. Because it
has twenty stories and was once one of the tallest

in the world, its walls had to be strong to support its great weight. Stone, of course, is very strong and, what's more, it looks strong. Its designer chose stone because the look of strength was important to him. As you can see, the Flatiron Building is very narrow. It is shaped like a thin wedge; your great-great-grandmother might have said that it was shaped like a flatiron. It is so narrow that its two long sides almost come to a point. A tall building standing on a sliver of land would have seemed weak and unsafe in the days before people were used to height. But the Flatiron Building doesn't look weak; it looks strong because its limestone blocks are deeply carved. The deep, regular carving tells us that the blocks are thick, and thick walls mean a strong building.

11

The Wilkinson Cotton Mill in Pawtucket, Rhode Island, was built in 1810 (11). It is small and it, too, looks strong. That solid look comes from the simple way its walls are built. Slices of stone are just gathered into rough layers. There is no carving; all we are shown is the natural face of the stone. That beautiful material and the clear design give the Wilkinson more dignity than many elaborate buildings have. The yellow building just to the right of the Wilkinson is the Slater Mill. It was built in 1793 and was the first cotton mill in America.

12

Here is still another building with walls of stone (12). It is a storage house in the old Red Fort, a few miles from the Taj Mahal (2). Its walls seem much thinner than the others we have seen. Although they are really quite heavy, they look light because the stone is smooth and the wall is very flat.

Look at the building on the right (13).

It is the East Building of the National Gallery of Art in Washington, D.C., and nearly every visitor to our capital comes to see it. Its pink-gray marble walls are smooth and perfect. At times the East Building looks as solid as the pyramids; at other times it seems to be a few sharp edges beneath a fine marble skin.

When stone walls are painted, surprising things happen. This old lighthouse at Pemaquid on the coast of Maine (14) often slips away into the sky. When the light is silver, the building vanishes.

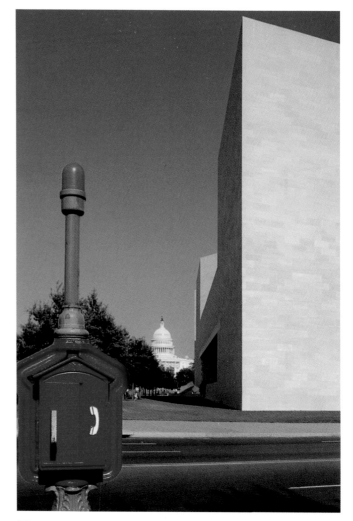

13

14

Rough stone joined by mortar made with bits of straw can make a wall look as though it is part of the earth. These houses are in Khunde, Nepal, a few miles from Mount Everest (15). They sit as comfortably on the roof of the world as do the great Himalaya mountains themselves. When materials are scarce, as they are in high mountains or on islands, they are used carefully. The best and most harmonious buildings are often the result.

16

Stone walls are tough and hard, but they bow easily to the tools of the stone carver. The carving can be as simple as columns and arches or as complicated as the face of the greatest of all English cathedrals, York Minster (16). While it has mystery and power, its carving is as delicate as lace. Order and loveliness at York have equal voices. The carving and the strong shape of the face flatter each other. The shape makes the carving seem finer, and the fine carving makes the shape more powerful. It is like the game of tag that we saw at the Brooklyn Bridge (7).

The John Hancock Tower in Boston is a wonderful glass building (17). It sits on the edge of an old square. Next to it is a stone church (55). Although the church is short and muscular, we would hardly notice it if it were dwarfed by the great shaft of a skyscraper. The designer of the Hancock Tower understood this, and he planned his building so that it would appear to change its shape as we move around it. From some places in Boston, it looks very slim. From other places, it looks like a block of thick blue ice turned on edge. And from still others, it is two crystal towers held together by a silver stripe. But next to the church, it thins into a quiet blue wall that pulls the sky down to the old square. There the stone church slumbers on like an old monk gathered up in his robes.

17

18

Metal walls sometimes remind us of glass. This is Citicorp Center in New York City (18). Most of it is covered in a layer of aluminum, and it looks like a silver bar on a violet-blue evening. When the sky turns yellow and silver-white, however, its fifty-nine stories slip quietly away into the sky.

This building is made of metal and glass, but it looks as though it is made of stone (19). It is the Haughwout Building on lower Broadway in Manhattan and it is assembled from cast iron. In the nineteenth century New York foundries made parts for buildings—columns and arches—out of cast iron. The parts were cheaper than stone but looked so much like stone that it took a magnet to tell them apart. The parts could be put together to make

19

20

buildings as handsome as those cut from the finest New England granite. Rows of columns, layers and layers of them, and arches marching on like soldiers, make a cast-iron building look very grand. Actually, most cast-iron buildings were factories, warehouses, and stores.

The shadows of the arches across the glass gave buildings like this one a rhythm—a regular dark splash skipping along a wall. While you may never have heard of the Haughwout Building, you have surely seen, in pictures at least, the most famous cast-iron structure in the world. It is the 130-foot dome of the United States Capitol (20). It was designed in 1855 and uses more cast iron than most cast-iron buildings.

21

Stucco is another beautiful and versatile material for walls. It can make a building look as fine, hard, and smooth as glass or as soft as a form that grew in nature. The town of Casares is in southern Spain (21), only a few miles from the coast of Africa. Along its narrow streets, you can almost smell that continent. The smooth stucco buildings of Casares are in southern Spain's own style and the town is one of the most striking sights on earth. Its clear, simple shapes and pure color are timeless.

When layer after layer of stucco is added to a building, its lines may disappear and a new, soft shape may emerge. Thick layers of stucco turn square corners in to round corners and straight walls into fluid, graceful forms. After years of such layering, the building will look almost as though it grew out of the earth. This is the Church of San Francisco de Asis at Ranchos de Taos in northern New Mexico (22). Like most of the old buildings in our Southwest, it is made of adobe—bricks that are dried in the sun instead of being baked in a kiln. The bricks are then smeared with layers of a stucco that is more clay than plaster. We are looking at the apse, or rear, of this Spanish mission church. Although it is

22

low, the apse and some of the side walls are held in place by supports called buttresses. Over two hundred years of layers have turned the buttresses and the walls into a single form that looks as if it might have risen from the desert and then been carved by the wind.

The Foundling Hospital in the old Italian city of Florence is also covered in stucco (23). Its courtyard was designed in 1419 by Filippo Brunelleschi to remind us of the splendid columns and arches of ancient Rome. While the courtyard doesn't really look Roman, its quiet, orderly design is as fresh as it was six hundred years ago. Its refinement—its pure, clear forms—comes from the slim columns and arches that play against the painted stucco in the spaces near them.

23

Stucco can also be carved. This is a double arch in a great fortress-palace in Granada (24). It is called the Alhambra and was built by the Moors almost seven hundred years ago as their time in Spain was nearing its close. The Alhambra is the Arabian Nights come to life. It is a place of Persian gardens, pools and fountains, courtyards, palace rooms, and strongholds that are fairylike and beautiful. Much of its beauty comes from the carved stucco that covers its walls and ceilings. It is so delicate and so intricate that it has no equal. Stucco makes the Alhambra another wonder of the world.

24

25

Concrete is an artificial stone—it is not natural like marble or granite—with a personality of its own, but it sometimes looks very much like natural stone. It can be cast into great slabs and fitted to make the walls of buildings like Habitat in Montreal (25). Habitat is a giant pile of apartments that shows the might of concrete. It is a strapping display of power.

The Trans World Airlines terminal at John F. Kennedy International Airport in New York tells us something else about concrete (26). It tells us that concrete will take soft, flowing shapes. The designer of the terminal must have loved air travel, because he gave us a building that looks as though it is sailing through air. Its roof sits on columns that sweep upward and its insides soar toward the heavens. When we enter it, we feel that our flight has already begun. Most terminals are the last place on land; this one is our first step into the sky.

Space is a part of the inside of a building. You can't touch it, but you know it's there. Habitat and the TWA terminal tell us about

26

27

more than just concrete; they tell us about space. Habitat holds space tightly between strong, straight walls. Most buildings do this. In the terminal, however, space seems to move: it flies in, roars around a bit, and then dashes off into the sky. With its space racing around corners, the TWA terminal is never at rest.

Brick is another wonderful material for walls. Because it is made of clay, it has the natural look of things that come from the earth, and because bricks are small, they can be used to build marvelous shapes. This is the great eight-sided bell tower of the Continental Mill in Lewiston, Maine (27). It is the corner of a cotton mill built more than a hundred years ago. Brick keeps the lines of the tower straight and gives the mill its dark, solid look.

28

In this row of buildings, brick wiggles its way along one side of Boston's famous Louisburg Square (28).

All brick buildings are not red. Some are as lively and as bright as painted wood. The Arthur M. Sackler Museum at Harvard University (29) uses layers of color to attract our attention to it.

29

30

31

This building is, of course, built of wood (30). It is a part of the old Pejepscot Paper Mill in Topsham, Maine, and its walls are painted clapboard. These are fishermen's shacks on Monhegan Island (31), a high rock ten miles off the coast of Maine. They are covered in cedar shingles. Finally, this building is at Sea Ranch (32) on the northern coast of California. It wears a coat of redwood boards that seasons of sun and sea have dyed black. All these buildings are very much alike because of their natural, easy feeling. They are in a simple style that we find all over America. It is a style that comes from our history, our land, and the way we live. Whether designed by famous architects or by the good carpenters who built them, their straight lines, the shape of their roofs, and their wood walls give them an honest, proud feeling.

Not all wooden buildings are as simple. The 1787 Meeting House in Rockingham, Vermont (33), is large, splendid, and very stern. There is nothing natural or easy about it—it looks strong enough to argue with the rocky hills of New England. The meetinghouse stands out against the nearby forest as proudly as the faith of the people who built it.

This is an enchanting wooden building (34). It is the Derby Summer House—a place to spend a few hours on a hot day. It was designed in 1793 for the garden of a gentleman named Elias Hasket Derby in Peabody, Massachusetts. As you can see from this small building, a very good architect can fashion poetry from buildings, just the way a writer fashions poetry from words.

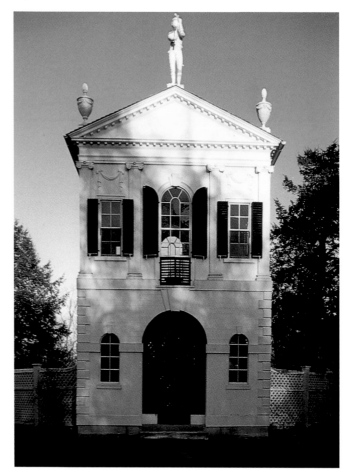

34

CHAPTER FOUR

Light and Color

Color is almost as important to a building as its materials. What color should a wall be? Before we think about this, we must remember that light lends color to buildings; when it changes, so will they.

These buildings are part of the Shaker Village at Sabbathday, Maine (35). On an afternoon in late winter they are warm and

36

37

creamy, but in December, shadows thrown at them make them look haunted (36). A building only a few yards away fades into the land on a hazy morning (37).

Strong sunlight often bleaches the things that it touches. The United States Capitol and the East Building of the National Gallery of Art are only blank shapes on a hot day (13).

This is the Baptist Church in East Hebron, Maine (38). It is blazing white at midday, but milky yellow at sunset.

39

In the rain, the golden Cathedral at Wells in England turns blue and green (39).

All but one of these buildings are pure white, but they often look as though they have other colors in them. It all depends on the weather, the hour, and the season. Changing

40

light changes color. When the sun is low, this old barn at Bristol, Maine (40), is redder than the reddest building in all of India, but if the day is dark, it is a dull, sad place. This house in Oxford, England, is a bright place on a dull morning (41). On a sunny day, however, a salmon door and pink walls look a bit odd in a stone university town.

41

42

The old Grange Hall in East Hebron, Maine (42), is just across the road from the Baptist Church (38). The Grange's paint gave way to the weather long ago. Still, the color of raw wood looks quite grand in that lonely place; it's as natural and comfortable in East Hebron as the simple stone buildings are in the valley below Mount Everest (15).

Sometimes a color has been used in a place for hundreds of years. Think of the fresh white of Casares (21). Sometimes a color has been on a certain kind of building—such as the white of old New England meetinghouses (33)—for a very long time. Those colors have become traditional; because they are a part of the spirit of a place, no other color will do.

43

CHAPTER FIVE

Pathways

Windows are pathways to the spirit of a
building (43). Some open a house to the world,
others shut it away. A wall gives a building
character, but windows help give it rhythm
and personality. They often tell us whether
we're going to like it.

This is the Palace of Winds in Jaipur, India
(44). It is an old building in an old pink and

44

45

red city. Its wonderful face has more windows than walls. Layers and layers of them turn the palace into a giant wedding cake. Although it is large, the delicate cases that hold its windows give it a joyful look.

Along one side of King's Mead Square in the English city of Bath stands this row of buildings (45). It is almost three hundred years old, the same age as the Palace of Winds. Bath is made of sets of buildings. Some form squares, some form half-moons, or crescents (81), and one set actually makes a circle. The row in King's Mead Square is calm and dignified, plain but

46

not dull. Because its walls give windows as much space as stone, we see a pattern of shapes forming, dark and then light and then dark again. Those changes from dark to light are like slow, steady music.

Moving light in a room is music that we can see. Here is a house that is more glass than wood (46). Because its windows open whole walls to the out-of-doors, more than light moves through its rooms. The sky and snowstorms, birds and the floating moon, come indoors too.

47

The old Moorish Baths of Granada are private places (47), sheltered from the out-of-doors. Small eight-sided windows high in the roof allow bits of light into the great stone hall. These windows are in the nearby Alhambra (48). They are fitted with screens made of pierced stone. Like spotlights, light coming through the screens strokes the patterns in the dazzling stucco. Most windows add movement to a room, but these add drama. In this chamber, a great performance is given every sunny day.

Doorways

Doorways, like windows, add personality to a building.

The doorway of the Ruggles House in Columbia Falls, Maine (49), has reached toward the main street of that small town since 1818. Its porch extends out to shelter visitors, and the slim windows that border the door allow a quick look into the house before

50

the door is opened. This doorway is a touch of cheer in a plain white wall. A year after the Ruggles House was finished, some of the citizens of Portsmouth, New Hampshire, built a private library for themselves. They called it the Portsmouth Athenaeum (50) and it is a private library to this day. It has a fine, carefully designed face, and its cannons and bronze plaques make it look quite grand. If we look at its doorway and then look back at the doorway of the Ruggles House, they seem much alike. Yet one building gives us a warmer feeling than the other. Part of this is because wood appears warmer than brick, but much of it is because of the Ruggles porch. Without a porch, the Athenaeum does not reach beyond its walls to offer shelter.

This is the entrance to El Tránsito, one of the oldest synagogues in Spain (51). Although it is pretty, it tells us very little about the house of prayer and study it leads to. Many southern European buildings hide behind their doorways. Plain entrances sometimes conceal fountains, gardens, and beautifully finished walls. However, as at El Tránsito, they may conceal rooms made simple and severe to encourage quiet thoughts.

51

52

This door is in Stow-on-the-Wold, England (52). It and the wall around it are almost as plain as those of the old synagogue and yet a coat of red paint has made a world of difference. That red paint tells us what is housed behind the door—a fire brigade.

These elegant doors have been on the front of the New Cathedral at Salamanca, Spain, for more than four hundred years (53). They announce one of the most serene and lovely

53

54

churches in Europe. The doorway of the abbey of Conques in the hills of France is even older (54). Almost a thousand years ago French pilgrims stopped there on their way to the tomb of St. James in Spain. Their trip was exhausting and dangerous. Along with rest, Conques offered the stern message carved in the arch. The fires of hell or the glory of heaven is our choice as we travel through life, it says; choose wisely.

This is a many-times great-grandson of churches like Conques (55). It is Trinity Church, the muscular church that sits next to Boston's John Hancock Tower (17). Its solid shape and round arches look very much like those in old French pilgrimage abbeys, yet it feels different. Its stone porch reaches out to draw us in. It has no stern message for the people of Boston.

Each of the doorways we have looked at helps form the personality of its building. Some doorways make the grand a bit more grand, some distance the building from the world, and some bring us cheer.

55

CHAPTER SEVEN

Looking Up

Do you look at the roofs of buildings? You
should, because that's where a building joins
the sky. A roof may slip quietly into the sky as
skyscrapers do (18), slice into it as Chartres
does (4), or even seem to push the sky aside.
This is the dome of the basilica of St. Peter's
in Rome (56). It is one of the most majestic
sights in the world. It was designed in 1546 by

57

Michelangelo and seems to sit like a king over that ancient city. It is so large that it has a life of its own, apart from the church below it. The church faces a great courtyard called a piazza. The Piazza of St. Peter's (57) is shaped like an ellipse—a not-quite-round circle. It's as if two giant hands had tugged at a once-round piazza and pulled it into a longer, narrower shape. The ellipse of the piazza makes the dome above it seem very solid. The tug-of-war between their two forms—forms that will last forever—is one of art's great dramas.

To see a roof we usually have to look up. Once in a while, however, we can look down on one. This is the nearly thousand-year-old roof of the wonderful Cathedral of Pisa in Italy (58). You would see it like this if you climbed its bell tower, the Leaning Tower of Pisa, for a

59

cockeyed view of the world. The sheets of lead on the long slopes of the roof and the half-circles below them form a handsome pattern of shapes.

This is another dome (59). It sits on a cathedral in the middle of a tangle of streets in Florence. You see it suddenly, like a mountain from a forest path, and then it seems to follow you. From then on, wherever you move in that city, at least a bit of it feels close by. After almost six hundred years, it is still a great architectural accomplishment.

Although it is a bit smaller than Michelangelo's dome (56), it is more than a hundred years older and even more beautiful. The long ribs and the delicate cupola cut it into eight wedges that are pulled upward and then held lightly in place by a white bow. Combining power and grace, it is the supreme achievement of that great architect Filippo Brunelleschi.

CHAPTER EIGHT

Old Bones
and New Bones

61

Even the beams and posts that hold a building together give it personality. This stone barn is at Lacock, a small English town (60). It may be five hundred years old. Its grizzled parts are like the bones of an old sea animal.

This framework holds the glass roof of the East Building of the National Gallery of Art (61). It is the visual opposite of the long, clear

62

lines of the outside walls (13) and reminds us that there is more to a building than first meets our eye. The East Building has a calm face, but there are places inside it, like this one, that spin with energy.

Fat columns have been part of this building for nine hundred years (62). We are looking at the great cathedral in the English city of Durham. It stands high above a river like a sturdy soldier. Bold Durham Cathedral is as much a fort as a church. Its stout frame—carved with rows of short lines—is as simple as its thick walls. There are no surprises at Durham as there are at the East Building, just a mighty form forever standing guard.

63

These arches are fans of white stone and red brick (63). The colors switch so quickly that the arches seem to roll. As you can see, this frame is very different from Durham's (62). Supporting the Great Mosque at Córdoba, Spain, the arches—pinched like horseshoes—roll from left to right, turning the mosque into an upside-down sea. A walk through Durham is sober and quiet; a walk through the Great Mosque is a trip through a thousand explosions.

Indoor Skies

65

A room is like a tiny world. Its ceiling is its sky. We are looking into Michelangelo's dome at St. Peter's (64). It is a vast indoor heaven, and space and light swirl through it.

The beautiful ribbing in this ceiling helps make King's College Chapel one of the most exquisite buildings at Cambridge University (65). The ceiling—in a style called fan

vaulting—is a gift from England's most famous king, Henry VIII. To turn stone into giant snowflakes is a miracle.

This is the inside of the dome of the ancient Pantheon in Rome (66, 87). The square panels sunk into it are called coffers and were once covered in gold. The dome is cast of concrete and in its center is an oculus—a Latin word meaning "eye"—that sends the sun on a tour of the coffers every day.

The Pazzi Chapel in Florence is another achievement of Filippo Brunelleschi (67). A portion of its shallow dome shows at the top of the photograph. The dome seems to float in the white ceiling because the green stone outlining it does not touch any other part of the building. The ceiling reminds us of a delicate drawing of lines, circles, and arcs that have been lightly touched with watercolors.

67

CHAPTER TEN

Ornaments

Fences protect property, but they are also
ornaments. Some fences call our attention to
the buildings they surround. At Ruggles House
(49), the fence directs our eye to the white
house behind it. The fence at the side of the
Cathedral at Seville is hardly a fence at all
(68). It's an excuse to line some handsome
forms along the edge of the vast church. This

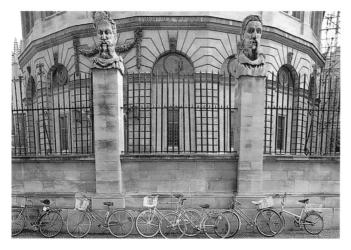

69

fence protects the Sheldonian Theatre at Oxford University from the public street (69). It also allows us to enjoy a lovely building designed by the greatest English architect, Sir Christopher Wren. The glowering faces on it are just part of a friendly joke.

This fence, however, is serious (70). It has become a wall to keep us out. Because it holds the inside in and the outside out, you have to stand on tiptoes to see the roof and delightful sculpture beyond it. It borders the old Roman Baths in Bath, England.

70

71

This is not a building with its belly sliced open (71). You are looking at a huge painting covering a blank wall of the Boston Architectural Center. It's an ornament that's truly fun to look at. The building has three lively sides; the fourth was once blank. Painting another building on it was a happy neighborhood act.

The pictures on this building—they are mosaics made of bits of glass and marble—are a necessary part of its design (72). We are looking at the face of the Cathedral in Orvieto, Italy. With thin shapes, sculpture, marbles, and rich carvings, it is bold enough to allow pictures to appear in its large triangles. Because the face is so rich, the pictures do not steal the show, nor are they out of place. They are just one part of one of the most joyous faces in the world.

73

CHAPTER ELEVEN

First Impressions

First impressions are very important. We often make up our mind about a building the moment we see it. Its setting—the land or water around it—is a part of that first impression. The Church of St. George Major sits on the edge of a tiny island, like a dot in a pale lagoon (73). It appears to be a mirage of domes and marble towers pushing up from the sea. It isn't a mirage, of course; it is very real. It's a building designed more than four hundred years ago by Andrea Palladio, but the illusion of rising up from the lagoon never quite fades. St. George Major will always be a place of first impressions.

The cliff dwellings at Antelope House Ruins in Canyon de Chelly National Monument, near Chinle, Arizona, are perched on a narrow sandstone balcony (74). A steep cliff rises up behind them. The cliff is so tall—perhaps a thousand feet or more—that it blocks the sky in the narrow canyon and so becomes a new sky: the reddish yellow of the rock face turns into a wrinkled and stormy heaven behind a flat plain. This lonely, haunting ruin,

abandoned by its Native American builders more than seven hundred years ago, is one of dozens scattered through parts of New Mexico, Colorado, and Arizona. Such cliff dwellings are among the most wonderful—and least appreciated—forms of American architecture. For those who visit them, the illusion of a sky with soaring folds is an enduring memory.

So we see that bits of land—a small island or perhaps a sheer cliff—are a part of our first thoughts about a building. The great square in the city of Siena is one of the noblest on earth (75). It is a giant scallop shell with old palaces perched on its rim. The first sight of them along the long red curve is unforgettable.

75

76

Our first view of the Royal Chapel in Granada (76) is across a pavement of small stones. Gray, white, and black, they spell out the coat of arms of King Ferdinand and Queen Isabella, whose tombs are in the chapel. The pavement tells us that we are coming to a quiet, thoughtful place—a place of rest for Spain's most famous citizens.

Shapes

Buildings come in many shapes. Some look the way they do because of what they do. Think of a lighthouse (14) or a windmill (77). A lighthouse is tall and slender because that is a perfect shape to hold a beacon high in the air. Lighthouses, therefore, look very much alike the world over. So do windmills. These stone windmills sit on a ridge in the middle of

Spain. The place is called Consuegra. One hundred and eighty-five years ago they ground wheat into flour. They were built with round walls so that their great vanes, which look like wings, could swing free in the wind and gather energy with which to turn the grinding wheels.

These buildings also look the way they do because of what they do (78). They are office buildings in Chicago. Because offices are really small boxes, these buildings hold the boxes together, layer upon layer, and so they, too, are shaped like boxes. But they are special boxes, three of the most special in our land. Together they are called the Federal Center and they were designed by one of the greatest modern architects, Ludwig Mies van der Rohe. At first

they may seem very plain. They have no ornaments—no paintings, no sculpture—and they are painted black, but the patterns made by the lines of windows and the light framework in the walls make us think about the beauty of straight lines, long planes, and careful proportions. Because they have no decoration to distract us, plain, clear buildings must be perfect in every way or we soon notice their flaws. Few of the tall buildings in our cities are so clear and perfect as these.

This building looks like a place in which to have fun (79). It's not an amusement park, however, but a vacation home for the prince who was to become King George IV of England. A jumble of make-believe Indian domes, Persian towers, and Chinese roofs, the

79

Brighton Pavilion was built for pleasant summers near the sea.

Some buildings look the way they do, not because of what they do, but because they embody their builders' attitudes. The Ruggles House (49) and the Rockingham Meeting House (33) were not built for summer pleasures. Their walls are plain and their lines are severe. They were built in stern times for serious lives and they show it.

This building is a palace and, like most palaces, was designed to be impressive (80). Built in Granada by a grandson of Ferdinand and Isabella, its outer walls form a large stone square resembling a fortress. Shortly after we enter the building, instead of finding halls

80

81

82

and chambers, we come to a courtyard, a great round space fitted neatly into the center of the palace. The sudden change from bleak stone walls to a round, light-filled space is grand drama.

This is one of the world's most perfect sights (81). It is a visitor's first view of the Royal Crescent at Bath. Marching along a great curve, it is a magnificent achievement in architecture. The parade of columns set on the heavy base, the lines of windows and the light top rail, form a pattern so orderly and elegant that it makes the Royal Crescent an ideal of stately beauty.

The white marble baptistery at Pisa (82)

and the Bodhinath Stupa in the Katmandu Valley, Nepal (83), represent other kinds of beauty. Instead of being calm and restrained, these buildings have elements that are full of energy. The baptistery is about the same age as the Leaning Tower—about seven hundred years old—and is only a few yards from it. The baptistery's short curves take our eyes up the round walls and onto the dome quickly and then back down again. The stupa is made up of a wonderful bunch of shapes. Its layers change from one form to another as they grow

83

from bottom to top. The changes keep our eyes moving and make us feel that the building is never at rest. The designers of the baptistery and the stupa did not select their designs because they happened to like energetic buildings. Their designs came from traditions that chose the designs for them. Some traditional designs are so splendid that they have been carried with ease from century to century.

The Parthenon (84, 3), the ancient Greek temple, is a row of columns holding up a roof shaped like a triangle. Nothing could be

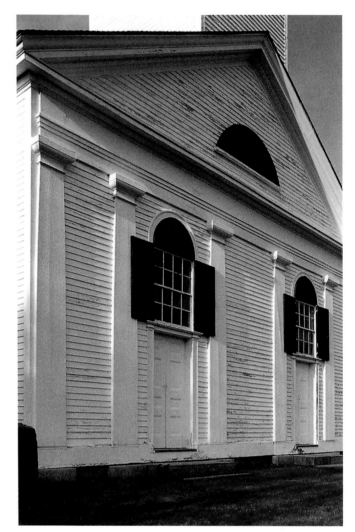

86

simpler—or more perfect. The columns point to the triangle and the triangle points to the sky. It is such a magnificent idea that it has come to stand for our noblest thoughts. It is also one of our oldest traditions. It appears in the old U.S. Patent Office Building of 1836 (85) and in the Universalist Church at Head Tide, Maine, built six years earlier (86). The face of the Parthenon has appeared so often and on so many buildings that it has become a universal symbol of refined beauty.

87

The Romans, who came after the Greeks, admired their ideas about beauty. Most Roman temples look very much like those built by the Greeks, but at least one takes us a step beyond them. In the Pantheon (87), the Romans started with a porch shaped like the end of a Greek temple, formed a circle of walls behind it, and then topped them with a huge dome. That combination—the porch and the dome—is twenty centuries old and timeless. The porch praises the dome and the dome leads the building in to the sky. Palladio used the

88

89

same combination in 1568 at La Rotonda (88), a villa on a hill on the outskirts of the Italian city of Vicenza. The amateur English architect Lord Burlington used it in 1725 in his Chiswick House, on the outskirts of London (89). And as you can see, Thomas Jefferson, our most gifted amateur architect, used it in the design of his lovely Monticello (90). The descendants of the Pantheon flourish the world over.

91

The Mormon Temple at Salt Lake City (91) and the Congregational Church at Harpswell, Maine (92), show us other traditions that have been carried down through the years. The Mormon Temple reminds us of the Cathedral at Chartres (4). After the year 1100, narrow cathedrals with roofs, spires, and towers drawn into sharp points rose into the skies over much of Europe. Light and airy, they soared over great cities, as the Mormon Temple does today. The temple's towers and windows are much like those at Chartres. The central doorway of the Harpswell church was inspired by the same cathedrals. The western portal, or doorway, of the Cathedral at York (16) is a graceful collection of pointed shapes,

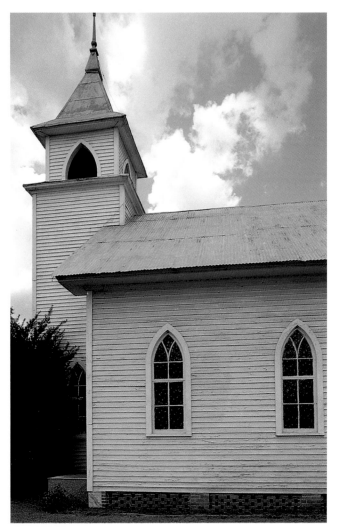

93

some rising side by side, some rising one within another. This is also true of the door at Harpswell. Like the one at York, an everlasting game is played here between order and grace. The plain wall of the wooden church turns the doorway into lace, and the doorway makes the wall into a white frame.

Finally, the simple buildings of the world carry on their own traditions. Some harmonize with nature; others contrast with it. This has gone on for generations without number. Like the fishermen's shacks on Monhegan Island (31) or the houses of Khunde (15) or this rural church in Wimauma, Florida (93), they follow one another throughout time.

There is no end to the story of beauty. We have seen that it has many forms and that new ones are added all the time. The new may seem strange at first, but if we are patient and willing to think about them, their wonder will appear. Like the grand buildings of history or the simple buildings that are close to the hearts of their builders, the new forms will share in the magic that comes from harmony. They will be works of art because their ingredients—their materials, colors, and shapes—will unite with their settings to lift us above the ordinary. That is what great art does.

A List

If you would like more information about the buildings and other structures in this book, here is a short list:

1. The Taj Mahal was built in Agra, India, between 1630 and 1648 by Shah Jahan, a Moslem ruler of India, in memory of his favorite wife.

2. A visit to the Taj Mahal should be at the time of the full moon.

3. The Parthenon was built in Athens, Greece, in 447–432 B.C. It was designed by the architects Ictinus and Callicrates and dedicated to Athena, the goddess of wisdom.

4. Chartres Cathedral is in Chartres, France. Part of it was built about 1145; the remainder, between 1194 and 1220. We don't know the name of its designer. Its style is called High Gothic.

5. Stonehenge is on Salisbury Plain in Wiltshire, not far from Salisbury, England. Its age isn't certain, but it is at least 3,500 years old. It appears to be a place for the worship of the sun.

6. The aqueduct at Segovia, Spain, is about two thousand years old and is a great example of Roman engineering. It is 2,392 feet long and so wonderfully built that it is still in use.

7. The Brooklyn Bridge was designed by John A. Roebling and was built by him and his son, Colonel Washington A. Roebling. Work began in 1869, the first wire was strung on August 14, 1876, and the bridge was opened on May 24, 1883. It crosses the East River to connect Manhattan to Brooklyn and is 1,595 feet 6 inches long.

8. The Pulteney Bridge in Bath, England, was designed by the great Scottish architect Robert Adam. It was built in 1774 to join Bath and Bathwick. It crosses the river Avon and is about 156 feet long.

9. The bridge at Ronda, Spain, was built about 1600. It crosses a deep ravine to bring together two parts of that ancient mountain town. Ronda is famous in the history of bullfighting.

10. The Flatiron Building is at Twenty-third Street in Manhattan, where Broadway crosses Fifth Avenue. It was designed by Daniel H. Burnham of Chicago and built in 1901. Its massive stone walls and the broad overhang of its roof, called a cornice, resemble those found in Italian palaces of the 1500s. Mr. Burnham's designs in Chicago include the plan for Grant Park, the Marshall Field Wholesale Store, the Monadnock Building, and a wonderful building called the Rookery.

11. The Wilkinson Cotton Mill was built in Pawtucket, Rhode Island, in 1810. Its designer is not known but it looks very much like other stone textile mills that were built in the early nineteenth century in Connecticut and Massachusetts. The designers of these mills were called "mechanics" and their later buildings, in brick, run north through New Hampshire and Maine. The Industrial Revolution—the great change from hand tools to powered machines and factories which began in England in the 1760s—first appeared in America in buildings such as the Slater and Wilkinson mills. As young people left New England farms to work in the mills, our cities grew, and from such beginnings we became an industrial nation.

12. The Red Fort in Agra, India, was built about the time of the Taj Mahal. Like the Taj, it is an example of Indian Muslim architecture, which is also called Mughal architecture.

13. The East Building of the National Gallery of Art in Washington, D.C., designed by I. M. Pei, was opened in 1978.

14. The Pemaquid Light at Pemaquid Point, Maine, was built in 1827. Like most American lighthouses, it is now automatic.

15. Khunde is a small town in the Khumbu Valley of Nepal—the route to Mount Everest. Its simple farm buildings are made of rough stone, often covered with a crude stucco of clay, sand, and a bit of lime.

16. The Cathedral at York, England, is also known as York Minster. Built between 1220 and 1480, it is the largest and most exquisite of all English Gothic cathedrals.

17. The John Hancock Tower in Boston was designed by Henry N. Cobb of I. M. Pei & Partners and was completed in 1974.

18. Citicorp Center in Manhattan is at 641 Lexington Avenue and was designed by Hugh Stubbins and Associates. It was built in 1977.

19. The Haughwout Building is at 488–492 Broadway in Manhattan. It was designed in 1857 by J. P. Gaynor and the cast iron was produced by James Bogardus.

20. The United States Capitol building is the work of many architects. Construction began on September 18, 1793, and, but for a few details, the building was finished in December 1863. Its most important designers were William Thornton, Benjamin H. Latrobe, Charles Bulfinch, and Thomas U. Walter. Mr. Walter prepared the plans for the cast-iron dome.

21. Casares is a white Spanish town called a *pueblo blanco*. It is a few miles inland from the southern resort area known as Costa del Sol.

22. The Church of San Francisco de Asis was built in 1772. While the Spanish settlers hoped it would look like the European buildings they remembered, much of its design comes from the pueblos of the Native Americans of New Mexico. In it we see two traditions joining to become a new tradition. The dignified mission churches of New Mexico are among our greatest national treasures.

23. The Foundling Hospital in Florence, Italy, is usually called the Ospedale. It was designed in 1419 by Filippo Brunelleschi and is the architectural beginning of the great period called the Renaissance.

24. The Court of the Myrtle Trees is in the fortress portion of the Alhambra, in Granada, called the Alcazar or the Casa Real. It was built in the fourteenth century.

25. Habitat was designed by the Israeli architect Moshe Safdie at the time of Expo 67, a world's fair held at Montreal, Canada, in 1967. Its style is called Modernist. Among the other Modernist buildings in this book are the John Hancock Tower (17), Citicorp Center (18), and the Federal Center complex (78).

26. The TWA terminal was designed by the architect Eero Saarinen in 1956. It is at John F. Kennedy International Airport in New York and is now called Terminal 5.

27. The Continental Mill tower in Lewiston, Maine, was designed by Charles F. Douglas and was built between 1871 and 1873.

28. Louisburg Square is on Beacon Hill in Boston. It was designed by S. P. Fuller in 1826. This row of curved-front houses was built between 1834 and 1837 in a style called Greek Revival.

29. The Arthur M. Sackler Museum in Cambridge, Massachusetts, was built in 1985. It was designed by the Scottish architect James Stirling and its style is called Postmodernist.

30. The Pejepscot Paper Mill addition in Topsham, Maine, was built about 1862. Its design has been credited by some historians to Samuel B. Dunning.

31. The fishermen's shacks on Monhegan Island, Maine, are like many simple sheds and storage buildings along the Maine coast.

32. The Sea Ranch Condominium was designed by Moore, Lyndon, Turnbull and Whitaker in 1966 for the Sea Ranch, a resort in Northern California.

33. The Rockingham Meeting House in Rockingham, Vermont, was built in 1787. It is the most impressive of the few New England meetinghouses still standing.

34. The Derby Summer House was designed in 1793 by the great architect Samuel McIntire of Salem, Massachusetts, for the nearby farm of a wealthy merchant, Elias Hasket Derby. The elegant figures on the peak of its roof were carved by the master shipcarvers John and Simeon Skillin, of Boston. The house is now at Glen Magna Farm in Danvers, Massachusetts, and its photograph appears through the courtesy of the Danvers Historical Society.

35. The Spin House (right) at Sabbathday (New Gloucester), Maine, was built in 1816. The Boys' Shop (left) was built in 1850. Both show the simple, pure lines of Shaker architecture.

36. This is another view of the Boys' Shop.

37. The Laundry was built at Sabbathday in 1821.

38. The Baptist Church at East Hebron, Maine, is very much like small, white wooden churches found all over the country. They are often designed and built by the very people who use them.

39. The full name of the Cathedral at Wells in England is the Cathedral Church of St. Andrew. It was begun between 1180 and 1240 and finished between 1290 and 1340. Its style, called Early English, is a type of Gothic architecture.

40. The barn at Bristol, Maine, was built in the years after the Civil War.

41. The house at Oxford, England, is a common English row house. The design of such town buildings changed very little between 1750 and 1850.

42. The Grange Hall at East Hebron, Maine, looks very much like the many grange halls that were built across America between 1875 and 1925.

43. The house at Bodhinath in the Katmandu Valley, Nepal, was probably built in the seventeenth century. Magnificently carved wooden window casings and screens often appear in the Katmandu Valley.

44. The Palace of Winds is in Jaipur, India. Jaipur is the capital of Rajasthan and was founded in 1727 by a maharaja named Sawaijai Singh, who was also an astronomer and mathematician. Jaipur is called the Pink City because its first buildings were built of a sandstone that ranged from pink to red. The later buildings were built of stucco that was painted pink. The women's palace, the Palace of Winds, is Jaipur's most beautiful building.

45. King's Mead Square in Bath, England, was designed by John Strahan in 1727.

46. This house is in Lewiston, Maine, and was designed by F. Frederick Bruck in 1960.

47. The Moorish Baths in Granada, Spain, were built in the eleventh century.

48. This chamber in the fourteenth-century Alhambra (also in Granada) is famous for its honeycomb-vaulted ceiling.

49. The Ruggles House is a beautiful white clapboard house in Columbia Falls, Maine. It was built in 1818 in a shape that is called "four square" because it appears to be perfectly square. It has wonderful interior carving.

50. The Portsmouth Athenaeum in Portsmouth, New Hampshire, was built in 1817 in a style similar to that used by Robert Adam on the Pulteney Bridge (8). In America it is called the Federal style. The Ruggles House (49) is a combination of Federal and earlier styles.

51. El Tránsito Synagogue was built in Toledo, Spain, in the fourteenth

century. It is one of the two remaining synagogues in that ancient capital of Spain. Both are now public monuments rather than houses of worship. The stuccowork in El Tránsito's interior is a famous example of Mudéjar decoration—the work of Muslim artisans.

52. Doorways like this one at Stow-on-the-Wold are found all over the British Isles.

53. The doorway to the New Cathedral in Salamanca, Spain, was installed between 1513 and 1560 and is an exquisite example of the architecture of the time.

54. The abbey at Conques, high in the mountains of southwestern France, is a famous pilgrimage abbey. Almost a thousand years old, it is an example of French Romanesque architecture.

55. Trinity Church in Boston, Massachusetts, sits in Copley Square. It was designed in 1873 by the architect H. H. Richardson in his own version of the Romanesque style. It is his best-known building. Richardson's influence was once very great throughout America.

56. The dome on St. Peter's in Vatican City was designed by Michelangelo in 1546. The style is called High Renaissance.

57. The magnificent curved piazza in front of St. Peter's was designed by Gianlorenzo Bernini in 1657. Its walls are formed by a pair of covered walks called colonnades. The colonnades seem to act as a pair of arms that reach out to draw visitors toward the enormous church.

58. The Cathedral at Pisa, Italy, is in the Pisan Romanesque style. Work on it began in the eleventh century.

59. Brunelleschi's dome for the Cathedral at Florence—it is always called the Duomo—was the first great dome erected after Roman times. It was designed in 1420, and when it was finished, the Florentines felt it was a miracle. It is still a miracle.

60. Tithe barns were built in the Middle Ages to hold the share of crops paid as rent by tenants to their landlords. This one at Lacock, England, is quite small but, like the larger ones, reminds us of the inside of a church.

61. The high ceiling of the East Building of the National Gallery of Art in Washington, D.C., and a mobile sculpture by Alexander Calder make a marvelous puzzle of steel and glass.

62. The interior of the Cathedral of Durham in northeast England goes back to the days of William the Conqueror. It is a splendid example of what is called Norman Gothic. It was built in the eleventh and twelfth centuries.

63. The interior of the Great Mosque at Córdoba, Spain, is a forest of pillars—some of which are Roman—and Moorish arches. It was begun in 785 and has been changed and enlarged many times over the centuries.

64. The interior of Michelangelo's dome for St. Peter's in Rome is so immense that it is difficult to appreciate its size. It is 137 feet 6 inches wide and 134 feet 8 inches to the inside of the lantern that crowns it.

65. The ceiling of King's College Chapel at Cambridge University in Cambridge, England, was installed in the sixteenth century. It is the finest Late Gothic vaulting in existence.

66. The dome of the Pantheon is 143 feet wide. The oculus sits 143 feet above the floor and provides a wonderful, even light for the ancient temple. The dome is the upper half of a circle. If the circle were completed, its lowest edge would touch the floor. This circle would be exactly the same size as the circle formed by the walls. These matching circles give the Pantheon perfect proportions.

67. The Pazzi Chapel is attached to the Church of Santa Croce. It was designed by Brunelleschi about 1430 and took thirty years to complete. The dome is about thirty-six feet wide. The brightly colored plaques at the base of the dome are by the Florentine sculptor Luca Della Robbia.

68. The Cathedral at Seville, Spain, is enormous, the third-largest church in Europe. Only St. Peter's in Rome and St. Paul's Cathedral in London are larger. The ceiling of St. Peter's—not including the dome—rises 150 feet above the pavement; Seville's Gothic ceiling rises more than 184 feet above its pavement. It was begun in 1401, and the portion in this photograph shows both Gothic and Renaissance styles.

69. Sir Christopher Wren was the greatest of all English architects. He designed the Sheldonian Theatre at Oxford University in Oxford, England, in 1664. This, and a few buildings like it, were to provide him with the training he would need for an enormous task that was to come, the rebuilding of London after the Great Fire of 1666. By designing more than fifty churches, including St. Paul's, and a grand customs house, he changed the face of that city forever.

70. This wall in Bath, England, separates the Roman Baths—Britain's finest Roman remains—from the Abbey Church yard.

71. This painting by artist Richard Haas added to a wall of the Boston Architectural Center looks like a gigantic version of the kind of drawings that architects have done for four hundred years.

72. The Cathedral of Orvieto (a hill city between Siena and Rome) was begun in 1290. Before it was completed, thirty-three architects had worked on it.

73. The Church of St. George Major is on the island of St. George in the Venice lagoon. For the most part, it was designed by the great architect Andrea Palladio and was built between 1566 and 1610.

74. Dozens of families lived at Antelope House between 1050 and 1300. Its builders, called the Anasazi, were the forefathers of the Pueblo Indians

of New Mexico, Arizona, and part of Colorado. The Anasazi were expert masons, and their work still stands in deep canyons in those states. The most famous of these cliff dwellings are at Mesa Verde National Park in southern Colorado. Abandoned soon after 1300, the cliff dwellings of the Southwest are incomparable in their lonely dignity.

75. The Piazza del Campo in Siena, Italy, is one of the great outdoor spaces of Europe.

76. Commissioned by King Ferdinand and Queen Isabella in 1506, the Royal Chapel was designed by Enrique de Egas and completed in 1521.

77. The center of Spain is a high plain. At Consuegra, however, a long hill pokes through the plain. Sometime around 1830 a line of stone windmills was built along its ridge. At times the windmills look like giants. An imaginary knight, Don Quixote, once fought an imaginary duel with windmills just like them.

78. The Federal Center complex was built between 1959 and 1973. It fills a block in Chicago bounded by West Adams Street, South Clark Street, West Jackson Boulevard, and South Dearborn Street. While the Modernist style takes many forms, it is buildings of this kind that we think of when we use that name.

79. The Royal Pavilion at Brighton, England, was designed between 1815 and 1818 by John Nash for the Prince Regent, who later became George IV.

80. The Palace of Charles V at the Alhambra in Granada, Spain, was designed in 1526 by Pedro Mochuca, a pupil of Michelangelo.

81. The Royal Crescent in Bath, England, was designed by John Wood the Younger in 1767. It took eight years to build and is the greatest single achievement in English urban architecture.

82. The baptistery at Pisa was begun in 1153 and completed early in the

fourteenth century. The lower part is Romanesque; the upper is Gothic.

83. The Bodhinath Stupa is believed to be from four hundred to five hundred years old. A stupa is a mound holding Buddhist relics and devotional objects. This one in the Katmandu Valley of Nepal is one of the largest in the world. It was severely damaged in an earthquake in 2015.

84. This is another view of the Parthenon.

85. During the early years of the nineteenth century, most U.S. government buildings followed the styles of ancient Greece and Rome. The Patent Office Building in Washington was begun in 1836 and is a fine example of the Greek Revival style. It was designed by Robert Mills, who also designed the Washington Monument and the Treasury Building. The National Portrait Gallery and the National Museum of American Art now occupy the old patent office.

86. The Universalist Church at Head Tide, Maine, was built in 1830. Its designer is unknown. It is partly in the Greek Revival style and buildings like it were built throughout New England in the early nineteenth century.

87. The Pantheon in Rome is the only perfectly preserved ancient building. It was first built in 27 B.C. and then rebuilt by the emperor Hadrian between A.D. 117 and 125.

88. The actual name of this building in Vicenza, Italy is Villa Almerico but no one calls it that. It is called La Rotonda because it's most important room is round and covered by a dome. With its four porches, dome, and beautifully placed sculpture, its quiet dignity has fascinated people for centuries. It has influenced buildings the world over.

89. Chiswick House was designed by Lord Burlington and William Kent in 1725. It is in a part of London called Chiswick.

90. This is the West Front of Monticello. It is in Charlottesville, Virginia,

and was designed by Thomas Jefferson in stages between 1770 and 1806.

91. The Mormon Temple in Salt Lake City, Utah, was designed by Truman O. Angell and Joseph Young and built between 1853 and 1893.

92. The Elijah Kellogg Congregational Church in Harpswell, Maine, was built in 1843. Its designer is unknown, but it is a beautiful mixture of Greek Revival and Gothic Revival styles.

93. The Methodist Episcopal Church in Wimauma, Florida, was built in 1913. Like the Baptist Church in East Hebron, Maine (38), it is one of many simple wooden churches that appear in rural communities throughout America.

About the Author

Philip M. Isaacson was an attorney and an art critic for the *Maine Sunday Telegram*. In addition to *Round Buildings, Square Buildings & Buildings That Wiggle Like a Fish,* Mr. Isaacson also wrote *A Short Walk Around the Pyramids & Through the World of Art*. He passed away in 2013. He was eighty-nine years old.